Calling Revealed: 7 Spiritual Lessons to Uncover Your Purpose

SHEILA HARRIS

Copyright © 2020 Sheila Harris

All rights reserved.

ISBN: 9798682313327

DEDICATION

This book is dedicated to those who are waiting to walk into their true purpose. I pray that you always listen for that still, small voice—and peace—to guide you on the path specifically tailored for you.

CONTENTS

	Acknowledgments	
1	Preface	i
2	Introduction	Pg 1
3	Lesson 1: Your Calling May Come at a Price	Pg 6
4	Lesson 2: God Will Use it All	Pg 10
5	Lesson 3: Don't Get Too Comfortable	Pg 20
6	Lesson 4: You May Have to Move Far	Pg 29
7	Lesson 5: …And You May Have to Move Quickly!	Pg 36
8	Lesson 6: Be Prepared to Sacrifice Something	Pg 40
9	Lesson 7: Last Call	Pg 43
10	About the Author	Pg 45-46

ACKNOWLEDGMENTS

This book is dedicated to my **Lord and Savior Jesus Christ**, who graciously took my place and gave me this great gift of salvation. It is my prayer that everyone will experience the true peace that only comes from walking with Him...

Mommy and Derrick: It's been "the three of us" since Daddy took an early flight (miss you Daddy.) But we can say that through God's grace and mercy—we made it. Mom: I thank you for your love, your many sacrifices, showing us strength in the midst of adversity, your sense of humor...and of course your great Southern cooking (wait... what time is dinner?) D: You are the BEST "baby" brother ever! Thank you for your constant patience, love...and making sure that there's always at least one dessert left for me!

To **my ENTIRE family** up North, down South, across the country and around the world (uncles/aunts/cousins.) I'm proud to come from such a rich legacy of strength, kindness and love.

Special thanks to the AMAZING publicist extraordinaire **Erma Byrd**. I greatly appreciate your Godly insight, constant encouragement, words of wisdom and most of all...the time you took to read the thoughts that were on my heart. You are truly a gem!

Mikki Taylor: Thank you for constantly pushing me to think bigger...and reminding me that God always multiplies!

Audrey Adams: I will always remember when you took a chance on me so many years ago. Your kindness will never be forgotten.

My entire Greater Refuge Temple/COOLJC Family, and to my Pastor, Bishop Charles and Mother Faye Wright, Sr., and Assistant Pastor, Bishop William and Lady (Dr.) Sarai Wilkins, Jr. Thank you all for your tremendous examples of Godly leadership and love. I also honor the memory of Bishop William Lee Bonner. Miss you always...

To my whole "Framily" (that's family who have become my best friends and friends who have become my family for life): I'm so thankful for the divine connections, the long phone calls, the prayers, the kindness, the laughter, the hilarious texts, the car rides...and especially the late night cookie runs! I love you with all of my heart!

Love, Sheila

PREFACE

What happens after the lockdown?

That's a question many of us hope to answer soon. At the time that I'm writing this, the entire world is on lockdown due to the COVID-19 pandemic. It's unprecedented, scary and at this very moment, we're not quite sure when it will all be over.

In the midst of this trying time, most of us are employing tactics that we've never had to before—such as "social distancing" or learning to "shelter in place." We've been limited in what we're used to doing on a regular basis—such as running to the grocery store or going out to dinner with friends and family. Everything seems like it's at a standstill at the moment. If you're like me, you treasure the time when you can connect with family and friends (even if it's only virtually or via our phones.) We are literally praying and pushing through this until the end.

During this season, you may have a lot of time to think and evaluate some things in your life. We are all believing that there will be life on the other side of this. The question is what your life or mine will look like when after we get through it.

After this lockdown, many of us will return to our jobs or careers and operate as we did before. It will just be business as usual. Then we'll continue that same trend for the next two, five or even ten years if we allow it. For some of us, that will be sufficient. That is, until another shift happens in your life. You may only see the time as an extended break and choose to keep the same pace and not rock the boat. However, you may also miss the fact that it also can be the perfect time to reevaluate your path and make some changes. You'll think about it for a bit. Then the time passes, and you go with what you know. So, the usual cycle continues, over and over. Year after year after year.

Tired yet? I know I am.

I am praying for a swift and speedy end to this season. But I'm also praying and taking a close inventory of my own life right now. Now, I've always tried to pay attention to the direction my steps are being led in, and the ultimate impact that I'm supposed to have along the way. However, our current situation has allowed me to dig even deeper.

Which brings me to what you're about to read here in, *Calling Revealed*.

You see, I believe that we're all born with gifts and talents that are meant to bless others around us. The key is not only recognizing and acknowledging them but moving forward and actually putting them to use.

Some of us have been blessed to recognize our gifts early on and to be able to cultivate them (or perhaps your parents or family did when you were very young.) Then there are those of us who didn't acknowledge or use our gifts until later on in life—either because we were not aware of them, or simply because we just let fear, or our own insecurities hold us back.

Regardless of your path and timing, I want you to take this time to really listen. Listen to your heart. Listen for that still, small voice speaking to you (we'll talk more about that later.) Most of all, take the time to recognize the calling that is on your life, and start taking steps towards it.

I hope and pray that by the time you read this, we would have made it to the other side of COVID-19. When we do, I want to see you moving and walking in the purpose and calling that God has designed for you.

I'll see you on the other side.

INTRODUCTION:

MAYBE GOD'S TRYING TO TELL YOU SOMETHING...

Scripture: Romans 11:29:

"For God's gifts and His call are irrevocable..." (NIV)

Have you ever felt like it was time for a change?

It may be from a job. Or a relationship. A neighborhood. Maybe even from your church or auxiliary position that you've held on to. The reasons will vary and can come from so many directions. Someone may have told you that you've been in one place way too long, so you should just move on. You're not moving up the ladder anyway, so what's the point? There's no fruit. You're not making an impact. Things are not getting better at all. Of course, the realization that you're not getting any younger definitely doesn't help matters. Sometimes you just feel like your life is out of balance by the weight of everything on your plate.

What's worse is that you're not sure what to do next. You may have tried to make your own power moves—widening your network, updating your resume, going on interview after interview, all in an effort to make things happen. But then, nothing works. The position that you were a top candidate for suddenly gets filled. Your once robust list of industry contacts has thinned out over time. The position that you flowed so well in before now doesn't seem to fit anymore. You know that you want a change, but not only are you unsure of which way to turn—but now it feels like there's actually something blocking your progress. Of course, you go through the process of self-reflection and examination; asking yourself questions like, "OK, it's me isn't it? What can I do better? How can I change?" However, even after that process is over, change doesn't come. To say this can be frustrating and confusing is an understatement. Like, seriously? What is happening here?

It's time to ask yourself different questions.

It is said that the definition of insanity is doing the same thing repeatedly and expecting a different result. While we may see others doing this, how many of us exhibit this same behavior unconsciously? What...not you? Let's be real for a minute. How many of you have relied on your job as your only source of income—whether through habit or necessity? But deep down inside, you know that there's an entrepreneur screaming to be unleashed! Unfortunately, you repeatedly ignore your instincts and push all of your amazing ideas back inside your head, because you want to stay safe. For most of you reading this, that's real. So you proceed in doing what's always been normal to you—whether it's inching you closer to your dreams or not. The hard part? You can't shake that little nudge...that something inside of you that's telling you there's something else for you to do...

That is the point of this book. It's to help you to recognize the fact that something has been calling you. To encourage you to not be afraid to do something different. To help you to realize that you literally will not be able to find true rest, peace and joy until you're walking in the purpose that was intended for your life. To help you to find your *real* assignment and purpose.

I will pause here to say that I believe in writing from a place of authenticity and genuineness. So trust and believe, many of the thoughts and questions you'll see reflected in this book have been asked of me by mentees, as well as industry peers during the course of my career. Honestly, after working in the public relations industry for over 25 years, I would be dishonest if I said that I've never asked myself some of these questions along the way! One thing that I try to remind others is that, no matter how old you are, class is always in session. That means that we should never stop growing and learning. It's also prideful to believe that you've got everything on lock. Trust me, mistakes will come at every point and stage in your life—from entry-level to the c-suite. What you have to keep in mind is what I call the 3R's: Recognize, Recovery and Restoration. **Recognize** that there is an issue and that you may need to make a change. Seek wisdom on how to *recover* from the immediate effects of a calamity or an unexpected decision (whether yours or someone else's). Then, learn to live in a spirit and mindset of **restoration**, where you have not let the sins, disappointments and hurt from the past to hinder and seep into your purpose-filled future.

Now, I know you're booked and busy. You've got a lot going on, and you don't have a lot of time. Understood. That's why I wrote this book as a quick teaching that you can read at your own pace. I will say that as a woman of faith, I try to use the Bible and the Holy Spirit for direction in every area of my life. So, I've included scriptures with situations that we all can relate to; all dealing with moving into one's assignment or call. Throughout this book, I wanted to keep the recurring theme of how a man or woman was happily living their life, until they were faced with a choice to do something out of the ordinary in order to be who God truly called them to be. For some, it was not an easy decision—especially when option #1 allowed them to be comfortable if they continued to stick with what was familiar. They each realized that in order to see a different result, they had to switch gears—even if meant taking a huge risk. In the end, it turned out in their favor.

I have to say that as I continue to age gracefully (aka get older!) I am still learning the importance and gift of keeping things real. So I want to warn you now, that the examples that I share in this book try to capture the emotion and heart of what each person was feeling at the time. This is so that you're not surprised and shocked in your own journey, when it seems like you just can't catch a break (you can read *1 Peter 4:12* for more on that.) For instance, when I refer to the conflict experienced by David, Joseph, Esther and others, I want you to imagine what it would feel like if you were in their shoes. Better yet, apply their scenarios to your own life! David's years of running from someone who was once a father figure to him may not be your reality. But can you apply what he must have been feeling at that time—the rejection, fear, confusion—to what you're going through? If so, then you can be encouraged by the fact that although his path to the throne was rocky, he was able to learn lessons along the way that carried him through the turmoil that awaited him in his later years.

Romans 11:29 states: "For the gifts and calling of God are without repentance." (KJV) Another translation says: "For the gifts and the calling of God are irrevocable." (NKJV) That means final. All of us are born with gifts and passions. If we're not careful, we can allow time, people and circumstances to push us further and further away from our purpose. But the Word of God states here that He does not change His mind about the calling and assignment for us. If you're stuck in some area of your life right now and wondering why you're not moving forward the way you thought you would, start to ask yourself why you're really here. Once you find out, you'll have a whole new compass to guide you to where you really need to be. And you won't be stuck for much longer. Let each of the examples in this book help to guide you on your own path.

Remember fam: there's something that you have that I need. I have something that you need. Your obedience to pursuing and fulfilling your assignment—launching your own business, building a new ministry, dropping an album, writing a book—may save someone's life. Think of it as a way to leave your mark on the Earth. Too much is at risk, and time is too short. So, don't ignore your call. Do it while sweating and shaking in your boots if you have to! But go forth in your real assignment and calling.

One last thing…I have another confession to make.

I found that this writing process to be prophetic in nature for me. As I mentioned, I too have sought and re-sought God for a change in my own life's trajectory. Over the years, I have felt a nudge when a change was needed. I eventually had to become honest with myself and finally admit that I needed to do something different—regardless of the cost and the change of mindset that it would require. You see, there were various times when it felt like I was bumping my head against the proverbial glass ceiling or an invisible block (more on that later on.) I was often puzzled as to why the formula that seemed to work for others wasn't working for me; or at least in the way that I hoped. Didn't I have the receipts? The experience? The contacts? The ability? One could argue yes. However, I was concerned that I wasn't seeing some of the more tangible rewards and fruit that I was expecting from the one tree that I was focused on. Trust me, I made sure that I shook down that tree for as much fruit as I could get out of it! Here's the problem: I was so focused on getting all of my fruit from just one tree, that I ignored all of my other God-given seeds. And there they sat day after day, year after year—just begging for me to plant them so that a new harvest could finally be created for me.

Friends, please don't make this same mistake. You should always remember that you are born with multiple seeds in your hand, and that new trees and fruit are available for you and I to reap in God's time. That's right...there is enough fruit available for everyone! But we have to be willing to leave behind our old thought patterns and ways—even if they worked well for us in a different season. Dare I say, I believe that God will not allow the tree that you're trying to shake down to bear anymore fruit for you, until you finally start paying attention to all of the other seeds He gave you and actually start doing something with them. Today.

As I try to encourage you with this book, trust and believe that He is speaking to me as well. No, my friends, you're not alone! We're definitely in this together.

So, let's move forward boldly and confidently as our true purpose, assignment and calling is finally revealed.

LESSON 1:

YOUR CALLING MAY COME AT A PRICE

King David's Story

Scripture: 1 Samuel 26:11

I mentioned earlier that as a woman of faith, I use the Bible to help me to tackle life's situations. I try to examine the experiences of each character, and how they both handled and eventually overcame their challenges. That brings me to the story of David.

I have to say that the story of the early years of King David is one of my favorite stories in the Bible that I continue to read over and over. Why? Well, because his tale is so intriguing and relatable, especially if we're talking about recognizing your calling—and what it will cost you.

If you read the book of 1st Samuel, you'll meet a young man who was described as being a man, "after God's own heart." That says a whole lot! Now just like us, David wasn't perfect. If you continue to read the books of 1st and 2nd Samuel, you'll see his mistakes on display. But regardless of whatever he did that was out of pocket, he eventually would repent to the God whom he served and truly loved.

In 1 Samuel Chapter 8, you will read how the children of Israel had pushed over and over for the prophet Samuel to give them a king to lead them. Samuel tried to warn them that having a king would just bring them a whole new set of problems—their sons would be sent to war, they would have to work the land, they would be taxed, and on and on—but they didn't want to hear it. So he gave in and eventually the Lord had him to anoint a young man named Saul as their king. At first things were going alright. Saul did his job well enough. Until one day, he decided to disobey Samuel (and God) by not fully carrying out the specific instructions given to him concerning dealing with Israel's enemies, the Amalekites. It caused Samuel to admonish him with the often-quoted phrase, "to obey is better than sacrifice" (1 Samuel 15: 22). God was so displeased with him to the point that he rejected him as king, and he told Samuel that he found someone else to take his place. That someone? David, the son of Jesse.

David's call was interesting to say the least. Yes, he was anointed to become king of Israel. Amazing right? Sure, but if you keep reading, it definitely didn't happen right away. He got the throne later on. But it came with a price. When the Lord sent Samuel to anoint the new king from Jesse's house, David didn't walk out with a new crown, a robe and money in his bank account. No, David went back to doing what he always did—tending sheep. In fact, it wasn't until after years of running from his one-time mentor, Saul, that he finally gained the crown.

I want us to really look at what had to be going through David's mind and heart during his early years. First, he never asked to be king. He was happy working in the fields tending his father's flocks. I won't dwell on the fact that when Samuel was sent to Jesse to anoint a new king, and asked to see all of his sons, David's own father forgot about him! The Lord had to tell Samuel not to be impressed by the outward appearance of the rest of David's brothers, because God looks at our hearts (*1 Samuel 16:7*). After that, God directed Samuel to anoint David in the presence of his brothers, and he left.

I always admired David's story because he remained humble on his path to the throne. As you read on in 1 Samuel 17, his life made a shift when he decided to confront Israel's Philistine enemy: the giant Goliath. Of course, no one paid attention to the little shepherd boy as he proclaimed that he would fight an enemy that grown men were afraid to face. But David wasn't afraid. He knew in his heart that, if God was on his side, he would win every battle. The rest is history—he took down Goliath and enjoyed the favor and accolades of his peers. Everyone could see that David was special and destined for amazing things. Even Saul's son, Johnathan, who actually was the rightful heir to the throne, was fine with David taking his position. David would have continued to enjoy the favor of the crowd, if Saul hadn't become jealous and determined to kill him (*1 Samuel 18:6-9.*)

Although David was a victim of a tyrannical king, he never once took advantage of opportunities to retaliate against Saul's attacks. He definitely would have been within his right. Instead, he just kept running from him. I'm sure David said to himself, "Hey! I never even asked for any of this. I was fine with just tending sheep! I'm not here for this. You can have it all!" No, David's only intention was to defend the name of the Lord of Israel when he went after Goliath. He was called to step up and step out. It was an assignment that he couldn't just shake off. So he accepted the call. He just didn't know that it was a call that would almost cost him his life.

I know that some of you can probably relate here. You may be approaching yet another anniversary of heading up a church ministry group or looking to make the next logical step in your career. You're settled on how you're going to move, only because it's in front of you and it's comfortable. You're cool. Until God starts to put a call on your life that causes you to acknowledge that a shift has to take place. Deep down inside, you know that you were called for something else.

If that's not enough, I believe the Lord won't allow you to progress on the normal path you plotted until you recognize that you were made for more. You may apply for a safe job, and may even becoming a leading candidate, until they suddenly tell you that the position went to someone else. Or, you may be expecting that after so many years of service, the next step is to lead a department that you believe you were made for. It's a great plan in your mind, until the economy dips and due to economic restraints the company now has to let you go (nothing personal.)

After a while, you begin to see a pattern. It's at that point, where you have to take a step back and re-evaluate your life.

Just like David, I can imagine not only the frustration you're feeling, but also the fear. To do the ordinary doesn't require much. You can dial it in without a lot effort, and no one will notice, because your work is spectacular. So, you think you've got it figured out, and the next step is what you see everyone else doing: continuing on the path of least resistance. Take your pick. Whether you're in pursuit of the next rung on the corporate ladder or serving in an area that you feel like you're not feeling passionate about anymore. Sometimes, we stick with it in order to avoid the tension that comes with going after your true purpose.

Friends, this isn't how we were meant to live. Just as David learned to trust in the Lord even more as he fled from Saul, you will also learn how to trust Him as you walk towards your calling, regardless of what's coming at you. As we learned from David, there will be moments of pain, hurt and confusion. But in the end, David wound up with the victory—and the throne. All because he knew that the best path to take, was the path the Lord set before him. A path of success and a legacy that lasted even until this day.

LESSON 2:
GOD WILL USE IT ALL

Joseph's Story

Scripture: Genesis 50:18-21

"Just throw it all away!"

Isn't that what most of us say when things don't go the way we expected? Whether it's a job, a relationship…even a year that you had high hopes for. We just want to toss it out and start all over.

But I want to challenge you today. Don't just throw the whole experience away…learn to let Him use the bad parts too.

I mentioned in my introduction that I would keep it 100 with you. So here it is: life, and the road to your dreams, will not seem fair. Sometimes, you may start to take things personally. You will actually start to believe that a memo went out (unbeknownst to you) directing everyone to block your path. It will feel hurtful and confusing. Until you realize…this really wasn't just about you after all. Yes, this journey—even if it has moments of tears, anger and frustration—can lead you to a greater destiny than you could ever imagine. Trust me, once you survive this, He'll show you how to use that messy, burning pain for a greater purpose.

And that brings us to the story of Joseph.

If you read Genesis chapter 37, you'll find Joseph living his best life. He was the favorite son of his father, Jacob, out of all of his brothers (who, of course, were jealous because of this and hated him for it.) He was also the first offspring of Rachel, the true love of Jacob's life. His father even had a special coat made just for him that he proudly showed off. Yep, Joseph had it made. To strain the relationship with his older brothers even more, he decided to announce two dreams he had. *(Note: As you read this book, I encourage you to follow along using The Message version of the Bible for a modern day take. I'm using the King James Version moving forward):*

<u>*Genesis 37: 5-11:*</u>

5 And Joseph dreamed a dream, and he told it his brethren: and they hated him yet the more.

6 And he said unto them, Hear, I pray you, this dream which I have dreamed:

7 For, behold, we were binding sheaves in the field, and, lo, my sheaf arose, and also stood upright; and, behold, your sheaves stood round about, and made obeisance to my sheaf.

8 And his brethren said to him, Shalt thou indeed reign over us? or shalt thou indeed have dominion over us? And they hated him yet the more for his dreams, and for his words.

9 And he dreamed yet another dream, and told it his brethren, and said, Behold, I have dreamed a dream more; and, behold, the sun and the moon and the eleven stars made obeisance to me.

10 And he told it to his father, and to his brethren: and his father rebuked him, and said unto him, What is this dream that thou hast dreamed? Shall I and thy mother and thy brethren indeed come to bow down ourselves to thee to the earth?

11 And his brethren envied him; but his father observed the saying.

Basically, the dream showed that Joseph would eventually rise above his brothers and his father one day. Well, his older brothers were done with him after that. I'm sure they thought, "Listen, he has definitely lost his mind. Does he really think we're going to just bow down like that...and to him?! Is he for real? And why won't Dad ever stop him? No, it's not going down like that!" So, they found a way to kidnap him and then sold him to the Ishmaelites, who eventually took him far from home to Egypt. Of course, his brothers hid their devious act from their father, and made it seem that Joseph was eaten by a wild animal. So, as far as Jacob knew, Joseph was dead. He would never hold his beloved son again.

As the years went by, Joseph must have felt like he was in a bad movie. Can you imagine his thoughts during that season? I'm sure he asked himself, "Wait. What just happened here? Did my brothers really just do this to me? Did they really hate me that much? It can't be that serious. You've got to be kidding me!" One minute, he has enjoying favored elite status. The next, he's thrown into a pit by his brothers—who by the way, were actually going to kill him until the older siblings intervened and spared his life. So they decided instead to sell him. Although he probably always knew that they didn't care for him, I'm sure that he didn't think they would ever take it this far. His screams and cries for mercy didn't matter to them. Suddenly, he was torn away from all that he loved--especially his beloved father and younger brother. He must have resigned within himself that he would never see them again. And what about those dreams of success that he had? What a joke! Why had life played such a cruel trick on him?

Genesis 39:2 says: *"The Lord was with Joseph and he prospered, and he lived in the house of his Egyptian master…"* That speaks volumes to me. Because when you look at the next few verses, it doesn't seem to be getting any better for him. One minute, he's put in charge of the house of an Egyptian official, Potiphar, who trusts him. But then Joseph is thrown in jail when Potiphar's thirsty wife accuses him of trying to get with her (after he refused her advances) (*Genesis 39: 6-20.*) But the Bible still says that God was with him. While in jail, he even found favor with the warden and other prisoners. When he prayerfully interpreted the dreams of two inmates (Pharaoh's cupbearer and baker), he asked the cupbearer to remember him and to speak on Joseph's behalf when he was released. But two whole years passed before he was given a second thought. However, remember that the Word said that God was with Joseph. He had a purpose for his pain that would come to light.

Let's take a look at what happens two years later, when his former prison buddy remembers the promise he made to Joseph after Pharaoh is troubled by strange dreams (I've excerpted the story here from Genesis 41):

Genesis 41:8-16:

8 And it came to pass in the morning that his spirit was troubled; and he sent and called for all the magicians of Egypt, and all the wise men thereof: and Pharaoh told them his dream; but there was none that could interpret them unto Pharaoh.

9 Then spake the chief butler unto Pharaoh, saying, I do remember my faults this day:

10 Pharaoh was wroth with his servants, and put me in ward in the captain of the guard's house, both me and the chief baker:

11 And we dreamed a dream in one night, I and he; we dreamed each man according to the interpretation of his dream.

12 And there was there with us a young man, an Hebrew, servant to the captain of the guard; and we told him, and he interpreted to us our dreams; to each man according to his dream he did interpret.

13 And it came to pass, as he interpreted to us, so it was; me he restored unto mine office, and him he hanged.

14 Then Pharaoh sent and called Joseph, and they brought him hastily out of the dungeon: and he shaved himself, and changed his raiment, and came in unto Pharaoh.

15 And Pharaoh said unto Joseph, I have dreamed a dream, and there is none that can interpret it: and I have heard say of thee, that thou canst understand a dream to interpret it.

16 And Joseph answered Pharaoh, saying, It is not in me: God shall give Pharaoh an answer of peace.

<u>Genesis 41:28-43</u>:

28 This is the thing which I have spoken unto Pharaoh: What God is about to do he sheweth unto Pharaoh.

29 Behold, there come seven years of great plenty throughout all the land of Egypt:

30 And there shall arise after them seven years of famine; and all the plenty shall be forgotten in the land of Egypt; and the famine shall consume the land;

31 And the plenty shall not be known in the land by reason of that famine following; for it shall be very grievous.

32 And for that the dream was doubled unto Pharaoh twice; it is because the thing is established by God, and God will shortly bring it to pass.

33 Now therefore let Pharaoh look out a man discreet and wise, and set him over the land of Egypt.

34 Let Pharaoh do this, and let him appoint officers over the land, and take up the fifth part of the land of Egypt in the seven plenteous years.

35 And let them gather all the food of those good years that come, and lay up corn under the hand of Pharaoh, and let them keep food in the cities.

36 And that food shall be for store to the land against the seven years

of famine, which shall be in the land of Egypt; that the land perish not through the famine.

37 And the thing was good in the eyes of Pharaoh, and in the eyes of all his servants.

38 And Pharaoh said unto his servants, Can we find such a one as this is, a man in whom the Spirit of God is?

39 And Pharaoh said unto Joseph, Forasmuch as God hath shewed thee all this, there is none so discreet and wise as thou art:

40 Thou shalt be over my house, and according unto thy word shall all my people be ruled: only in the throne will I be greater than thou.

41 And Pharaoh said unto Joseph, See, I have set thee over all the land of Egypt.

42 And Pharaoh took off his ring from his hand, and put it upon Joseph's hand, and arrayed him in vestures of fine linen, and put a gold chain about his neck;

43 And he made him to ride in the second chariot which he had; and they cried before him, Bow the knee: and he made him ruler over all the land of Egypt.

Whew! Did you just read that? After all the pain that he went through, Joseph became ruler of Egypt. Only Pharaoh was above him in rank. Oh...*and* he was also given a wife and riches. The bible said that by this time, he was 30 years old. Of course, if the story ended there, one could argue that the promotion and the riches were the reward for the years of pain he endured being separated from his family and his father.

Spoiler alert—the story doesn't end there for Joseph. Remember what I said earlier: God can use it all. Even the painful parts.

In Genesis 42: 1-17, the story then shifts to Joseph's father Jacob (who by that time was very old) and his brothers back home, who are all trying to figure out how they're going to survive. As we read earlier, Pharaoh's dream showed seven years of plenty and seven years of lack. Well, they were now living out that dream in real time. The famine was definitely severe and reached where Jacob was. Finally, Jacob tells his older sons to go to Egypt to buy corn for them to eat before they all starved to death. So, they followed their father's instructions. However, when the brothers arrive, they ran into an expected situation.

<u>*Genesis 42:1-8:*</u>

1 Now when Jacob saw that there was corn in Egypt, Jacob said unto his sons, Why do ye look one upon another?

2 And he said, Behold, I have heard that there is corn in Egypt: get you down thither, and buy for us from thence; that we may live, and not die.

3 And Joseph's ten brethren went down to buy corn in Egypt.

4 But Benjamin, Joseph's brother, Jacob sent not with his brethren; for he said, Lest peradventure mischief befall him.

5 And the sons of Israel came to buy corn among those that came: for the famine was in the land of Canaan.

6 And Joseph was the governor over the land, and he it was that sold to all the people of the land: and Joseph's brethren came, and bowed down themselves before him with their faces to the earth.

7 And Joseph saw his brethren, and he knew them, but made himself strange unto them, and spake roughly unto them; and he said unto them, Whence come ye? And they said, From the land of Canaan to buy food.

8 And Joseph knew his brethren, but they knew not him.

Whoa. Talk about a plot twist! After all these years, Joseph—in a seat of power—comes face to face with the very ones who put him on the path of what was designed to be his destruction. And they didn't even recognize him (because he spoke through an interpreter.) The story goes on to describe how Joseph treats his brothers as they made their request for food. They were literally afraid of this high-ranking figure who seemed to hold their very fate in his hands:

<u>Genesis 42:9-17:</u>

9 And Joseph remembered the dreams which he dreamed of them, and said unto them, Ye are spies; to see the nakedness of the land ye are come.

10 And they said unto him, Nay, my lord, but to buy food are thy servants come.

11 We are all one man's sons; we are true men, thy servants are no spies.

12 And he said unto them, Nay, but to see the nakedness of the land ye are come.

13 And they said, Thy servants are twelve brethren, the sons of one man in the land of Canaan; and, behold, the youngest is this day with our father, and one is not.

14 And Joseph said unto them, That is it that I spake unto you, saying, Ye are spies:

15 Hereby ye shall be proved: By the life of Pharaoh ye shall not go forth hence, except your youngest brother come hither.

16 Send one of you, and let him fetch your brother, and ye shall be kept in prison, that your words may be proved, whether there be any truth in you: or else by the life of Pharaoh surely ye are spies.

17 And he put them all together into ward three days. Now, Joseph only went but so far with this. When he couldn't take it anymore, he finally revealed himself to them:

<u>Genesis 45:1-8:</u>

1 Then Joseph could not refrain himself before all them that stood by him; and he cried, Cause every man to go out from me. And there stood no man with him, while Joseph made himself known unto his brethren.

2 And he wept aloud: and the Egyptians and the house of Pharaoh heard.

3 And Joseph said unto his brethren, I am Joseph; doth my father yet live? And his brethren could not answer him; for they were troubled at his presence.

4 And Joseph said unto his brethren, Come near to me, I pray you. And they came near. And he said, I am Joseph your brother, whom ye sold into Egypt.

5 Now therefore be not grieved, nor angry with yourselves, that ye sold me hither: for God did send me before you to preserve life.

6 For these two years hath the famine been in the land: and yet there are five years, in the which there shall neither be earing nor harvest.

7 And God sent me before you to preserve you a posterity in the earth, and to save your lives by a great deliverance.

8 So now it was not you that sent me hither, but God: and he hath made me a father to Pharaoh, and lord of all his house, and a ruler throughout all the land of Egypt.

Let's pause for a minute. After all those years, Father Jacob was able to hold his beloved son in his arms once more. Not only that, he and Joseph's brothers were able to remain in Egypt until he was buried decades later.

The interesting thing to keep in mind is what happens right before their father passes. His older brothers wrestled with guilt for so long, and assumed that as soon as Father Jacob closed his eyes, Joseph would really let them have it. But Joseph had a message for all of them:

<u>*Genesis 50:15-21:*</u>

15 And when Joseph's brethren saw that their father was dead, they said, Joseph will peradventure hate us, and will certainly requite us all the evil which we did unto him.

16 And they sent a messenger unto Joseph, saying, Thy father did command before he died, saying,

17 So shall ye say unto Joseph, Forgive, I pray thee now, the trespass of thy brethren, and their sin; for they did unto thee evil: and now, we pray thee, forgive the trespass of the servants of the God of thy father. And Joseph wept when they spake unto him.

18 And his brethren also went and fell down before his face; and they said, Behold, we be thy servants.

19 And Joseph said unto them, Fear not: for am I in the place of God?

20 But as for you, ye thought evil against me; but God meant it unto good, to bring to pass, as it is this day, to save much people alive.

21 Now therefore fear ye not: I will nourish you, and your little ones. And he comforted them, and spake kindly unto them.

Do you see that in the end, God never forgot his promise and purpose for Joseph? He was sent ahead of his family so that all those years later, he would be able to save them from the famine.

That is what I want to remind you: God will even use the parts that you think are devastating for your good. The pain and tears are never lost on Him. He keeps a record, and when He's ready He will show not only you, but the world, that you are His child and His purpose for your life will be accomplished.

LESSON 3:
DON'T GET TOO COMFORTABLE

Queen Esther's Story

Scripture: Esther 4:12-14

You can never get too comfortable. Sometimes you have to speak up.

I know. It's really much easier to fly under the radar. Who wants the stress of sticking their neck out? You think, "If a situation is not hitting my neck of the woods, then there's no need for me to cause myself any extra trouble. So, I'll just lay low and hope nothing hits my direction..."

Sound familiar? The truth is, many of us have had moments like this. Especially when faced with something that may not directly affect us at the moment, but we have the power to intervene. Wrestling with those feelings is not the problem—it's how we'll proceed to handle the issue that's the bigger question. I will say that I had to learn that running from confrontation at any cost is never the answer. Because at some point, the challenge that's hitting your neighbor may eventually make its way to you. Which brings us to the story of Queen Esther.

In the beginning of the story, we find that Esther—a beautiful young Jewish woman who was raised as an orphaned child by her loving uncle Mordecai—found herself in the running to become queen. Her predecessor, Vashti, held the title until she disobeyed a command from her husband, King Xerxes. What was the command that she refused to comply with? Parading and dancing around him and his drunken friends at the latest royal party. Let's just say, it did not end well when she refused. After Vashti lost her title, the King and his advisors decided to hold a nationwide version of The Bachelor (starring himself) to help him find a new queen. Now, when Mordecai heard about this, he allowed Esther to be considered:

Esther 2:1-10:

2 After these things, when the wrath of king Ahasuerus was appeased, he remembered Vashti, and what she had done, and what was decreed against her.

2 Then said the king's servants that ministered unto him, Let there be fair young virgins sought for the king:

3 And let the king appoint officers in all the provinces of his kingdom, that they may gather together all the fair young virgins unto Shushan the palace, to the house of the women, unto the custody of Hege the king's chamberlain, keeper of the women; and let their things for purification be given them:

4 And let the maiden which pleaseth the king be queen instead of Vashti. And the thing pleased the king; and he did so.

5 Now in Shushan the palace there was a certain Jew, whose name was Mordecai, the son of Jair, the son of Shimei, the son of Kish, a Benjamite;

6 Who had been carried away from Jerusalem with the captivity which had been carried away with Jeconiah king of Judah, whom Nebuchadnezzar the king of Babylon had carried away.

7 And he brought up Hadassah, that is, Esther, his uncle's daughter: for she had neither father nor mother, and the maid was fair and beautiful; whom Mordecai, when her father and mother were dead, took for his own daughter.

8 So it came to pass, when the king's commandment and his decree was heard, and when many maidens were gathered together unto Shushan the palace, to the custody of Hegai, that Esther was brought also unto the king's house, to the custody of Hegai, keeper of the women.

9 And the maiden pleased him, and she obtained kindness of him; and he speedily gave her her things for purification, with such things as belonged to her, and seven maidens, which were meet to be given her, out of the king's house: and he preferred her and her maids unto the best place of the house of the women.

10 Esther had not shewed her people nor her kindred: for Mordecai had charged her that she should not shew it.

As you continue to read the story, you'll see that throughout the process, Esther received favor everywhere she went. From the officials in charge of all of the contestants, all the way up to the king himself. But note what verse 10 says above. The Message Bible version says: *"Esther didn't say anything about her family and racial background because Mordecai had told her not to..."* During the entire process, only she and Mordecai knew who she really was. This was in order to protect her. So she obeyed. Esther became queen, and her life was grand.

Until all of a sudden, her whole world was shaken up.

The king promoted a new official named Haman, who was above all the princes that were there. He was so high up in rank that the king even commanded that all should bow and reverence Haman as he walked by. (*Esther 3:1-2*) The Bible also notes that Haman was "the son of Hammedatha the Agagite." Translation: he was a descendant of Agag—one of Israel's staunchest enemies. His presence would mean bad news for the Jews living in the region. It turned out to be worse than anyone could imagine: Haman made a decree to destroy all the Jews in the kingdom. He also had the king to co-sign it, which meant it was a done deal.

And all the while, a Jewish queen sat quietly on the throne.

One person who wasn't going to stay quiet was Uncle Mordecai. He saw this as a 911 situation. Someone had to do something! He fasted, prayed and cried out. He went as far as he could to the king's gate. Sure enough, his niece and her staff heard him, but didn't know what the crying was all about. They tried to calm him down by sending clothing and such, but he wasn't having it. He sent a message to his niece with an update on the terror that was about to take place, admonishing her to go to the king on her people's behalf:

Esther 4:1-12:

1 When Mordecai perceived all that was done, Mordecai rent his clothes, and put on sackcloth with ashes, and went out into the midst of the city, and cried with a loud and a bitter cry;

2 And came even before the king's gate: for none might enter into the king's gate clothed with sackcloth.

3 And in every province, whithersoever the king's commandment and his decree came, there was great mourning among the Jews, and fasting, and weeping, and wailing; and many lay in sackcloth and ashes.

4 So Esther's maids and her chamberlains came and told it her. Then was the queen exceedingly grieved; and she sent raiment to clothe Mordecai, and to take away his sackcloth from him: but he received it not.

5 Then called Esther for Hatach, one of the king's chamberlains, whom he had appointed to attend upon her, and gave him a commandment to Mordecai, to know what it was, and why it was.

6 So Hatach went forth to Mordecai unto the street of the city, which was before the king's gate.

7 And Mordecai told him of all that had happened unto him, and of the sum of the money that Haman had promised to pay to the king's treasuries for the Jews, to destroy them.

8 Also he gave him the copy of the writing of the decree that was given at Shushan to destroy them, to shew it unto Esther, and to declare it unto her, and to charge her that she should go in unto the king, to make supplication unto him, and to make request before him for her people.

9 And Hatach came and told Esther the words of Mordecai.

10 Again Esther spake unto Hatach, and gave him commandment unto Mordecai;

11 All the king's servants, and the people of the king's provinces, do know, that whosoever, whether man or women, shall come unto the king into the inner court, who is not called, there is one law of his to put him to death, except such to whom the king shall hold out the golden sceptre, that he may live: but I have not been called to come in unto the king these thirty days.

12 And they told to Mordecai Esther's words.

As I said before, put yourself in each of these scenarios as you read. Your situation may not be as drastic as this. But consider your present role wherever you are. Are you helping to make a difference? Speaking up for others, even if it's not really your problem? Making things a little easier for your colleagues, employees or even your higher-ups? Better yet, can you discern when a storm is coming your way—and are you making preparations to face it? Or will you just wait until it hits your front door?

I can clearly remember times in my life where I stayed too quiet during a situation. Sometimes it was because I thought that my input would not make too much of a difference on the eventual outcome—especially if I attempted to do all that I could ahead of time. Other times it was to avoid a conflict or confrontation. Then there were times that I simply thought it would all work itself out in the end. Regardless of the scenario, I had to learn that most problems will not just go away. Sometimes they will even fester and multiply, if we don't address them immediately or destroy the root cause of it. I eventually learned to ask God to show me how to deal with issues head on—and even how to anticipate potential problems ahead of time, so that I could be better prepared. I can say that He has definitely helped me with this on so many levels. That doesn't mean that I don't get caught off guard sometimes! But the great thing is, nothing is ever a surprise to God. Through it all, I just ask Him to please give me clean hands and a pure heart (Psalm 24:4) so that I'll not only be ready for the fight, but I'll receive the lesson from the test that I was assigned to learn.

OK, back to Esther...

Uncle Mordecai explained to Esther why she shouldn't just turn a blind eye to what was going on around her. He understood her stance that, even in her role as Queen, going to the King uninvited wasn't something to be taken lightly. The King could literally order her to be killed. She absolutely had a right to be afraid of the mere thought of approaching him about this. But Mordecai's admonition brought her back to reality:

Esther 4:12-17:

12 And they told to Mordecai Esther's words.

13 Then Mordecai commanded to answer Esther, Think not with thyself that thou shalt escape in the king's house, more than all the Jews.

14 For if thou altogether holdest thy peace at this time, then shall there enlargement and deliverance arise to the Jews from another place; but thou and thy father's house shall be destroyed: and who knoweth whether thou art come to the kingdom for such a time as this?

15 Then Esther bade them return Mordecai this answer,

16 Go, gather together all the Jews that are present in Shushan, and fast ye for me, and neither eat nor drink three days, night or day: I also and my maidens will fast likewise; and so will I go in unto the king, which is not according to the law: and if I perish, I perish.

17 So Mordecai went his way, and did according to all that Esther had commanded him.

"If I perish, I perish." It's not easy to come to that resolution. Let's be clear: Esther could have left it all alone. She even could have offered to have Uncle Mordecai stay at the guest house until the current danger passed them by. However, something inside her knew that wouldn't be right. She began to understand that her role as Queen was bigger than her. She had to at least try to stand up for her people—even at the risk of losing her very life. So, she did:

<u>Esther 7: 1-10:</u>

1 So the king and Haman came to banquet with Esther the queen.

2 And the king said again unto Esther on the second day at the banquet of wine, What is thy petition, queen Esther? and it shall be granted thee: and what is thy request? and it shall be performed, even to the half of the kingdom.

3 Then Esther the queen answered and said, If I have found favour in thy sight, O king, and if it please the king, let my life be given me at my petition, and my people at my request:

4 For we are sold, I and my people, to be destroyed, to be slain, and to perish. But if we had been sold for bondmen and bondwomen, I had held my tongue, although the enemy could not countervail the king's damage.

5 Then the king Ahasuerus answered and said unto Esther the queen, Who is he, and where is he, that durst presume in his heart to do so?

6 And Esther said, The adversary and enemy is this wicked Haman. Then Haman was afraid before the king and the queen.

7 And the king arising from the banquet of wine in his wrath went into the palace garden: and Haman stood up to make request for his life to Esther the queen; for he saw that there was evil determined against him by the king.

8 Then the king returned out of the palace garden into the place of the

banquet of wine; and Haman was fallen upon the bed whereon Esther was. Then said the king, Will he force the queen also before me in the house? As the word went out of king's mouth, they covered Haman's face.

9 And Harbonah, one of the chamberlains, said before the king, Behold also, the gallows fifty cubits high, which Haman had made for Mordecai, who spoken good for the king, standeth in the house of Haman. Then the king said, Hang him thereon.

10 So they hanged Haman on the gallows that he had prepared for Mordecai. Then was the king's wrath pacified.

Haman's evil plot was uncovered! Esther's boldness allowed her people to have a fighting chance against their enemy. And in the end, they all got the victory: Esther remained Queen, and Mordecai even became prime minister and had authority next to the king.

Won't He do it?

Friend, I want you to know that there will be moments when speaking up and taking a risk is absolutely necessary in order to walk into your appointed assignment. But have no fear. Just like Esther, your steps will be divinely ordered as you stand up to your giant and do what you were called to do.

LESSON 4:
YOU MAY HAVE TO MOVE FAR

Ruth and Abraham's Story

Scripture: Ruth 1:16-19

Would you move to a new place for your call?

Many of us who are contemplating the next phase of our lives tend not to think out of the box. We only consider what's right in front of us. Or, we mirror the examples that we grew up with or were influenced by. The danger here is that our definition of success may be too short-sighted. For instance, we may think that our success or win will be found in the same neighborhood, company, ministry or industry that we have stayed in for five, ten, fifteen or twenty-five years. But what if God is trying to show you that where you need to be is far from home? That your season in the place where you are has now passed? And that in order to walk in the true place that He has for you, it will require you to simply...move? Would you still be willing to go?

I want us to look at two examples for this lesson: Ruth and Abraham. While their stories and paths are different, the context is the same. Most of all, I want you to pay attention to the fact that after they accepted their call, their lives became more blessed than they could ever imagine.

In the story of Ruth, we find a young woman who has gone through one of the most devastating moments anyone could ever experience. The Bible tells us in the first chapter of Ruth that a woman named Naomi and her husband, Elimelech, left their home in Bethlehem-judah to find food after a famine hit the land. They traveled to the country of Moab with their two sons and lived there for ten years. During that time, their sons married women of the land: Ruth and Orpah. Then life took a cruel turn. Elimelech passes, followed by his two sons tragically. Which left Naomi and her two daughters-in-law to figure out life moving forward. Naomi was not only saddened, but as a widow without any men in the house to support her during those times, she knew they would not make it. Although she loved Ruth and Orpah like her own daughters, she told them to move on with their lives. They were still young, so they could find new husbands to take care of them in their own land. Naomi, on the other hand, resigned herself to return to Bethlehem-judah on her own. This sounded like a reasonable solution for all.

Except, Ruth wasn't having it.

Somehow, the ways of her mother-in-law grew on the Moabitess woman. I believe Naomi, who at first probably didn't understand the ways or the culture of the women her sons married, showed so much kindness to Ruth and Orpah that it left a huge impression on their hearts. They became family. Also, I believe Naomi shared stories of the goodness of the God of Abraham, Isaac and Jacob with the young Moabite women. So, although the advice that Naomi gave them was practical, it didn't change how they felt about her. Eventually, Orpah decided to make a difficult choice in order to survive, and tearfully kissed her and said good-bye. Ruth, on the other hand, put up a fight:

Ruth 1: 8-19:

8 And Naomi said unto her two daughters in law, Go, return each to her mother's house: the Lord deal kindly with you, as ye have dealt with the dead, and with me.

9 The Lord grant you that ye may find rest, each of you in the house of her husband. Then she kissed them; and they lifted up their voice, and wept.

10 And they said unto her, Surely we will return with thee unto thy people.

11 And Naomi said, Turn again, my daughters: why will ye go with me? are there yet any more sons in my womb, that they may be your husbands?

12 Turn again, my daughters, go your way; for I am too old to have an husband. If I should say, I have hope, if I should have an husband also to night, and should also bear sons;

13 Would ye tarry for them till they were grown? would ye stay for them from having husbands? nay, my daughters; for it grieveth me much for your sakes that the hand of the Lord is gone out against me.

14 And they lifted up their voice, and wept again: and Orpah kissed her mother in law; but Ruth clave unto her.

15 And she said, Behold, thy sister in law is gone back unto her people, and unto her gods: return thou after thy sister in law.

16 And Ruth said, Intreat me not to leave thee, or to return from following after thee: for whither thou goest, I will go; and where thou lodgest, I will lodge: thy people shall be my people, and thy God my God:

17 Where thou diest, will I die, and there will I be buried: the Lord do so to me, and more also, if ought but death part thee and me.

18 When she saw that she was stedfastly minded to go with her, then she left speaking unto her.

19 So they two went until they came to Bethlehem. And it came to pass, when they were come to Bethlehem, that all the city was moved about them, and they said, Is this Naomi?

While the story of Ruth is always referred to in reference to someone who "found her Boaz," I want us to look deeper here. Here is a young woman who is faced with the decision of a lifetime. Should she stay where she is—while still mourning the death of her husband—and take her chances in a place where she's comfortable? Or, should she venture out with a woman whose spirit has touched her heart and follow her—and the God that she's heard so much about? I mean, there were no guarantees either way. Naomi was old, so she would more than likely be the one taking care of her mother-in-law. But if you read her words, "not even death itself is going to come between us," we can see that she was clearly sold out—she was going with Naomi.

Of course, we know the highlights of Ruth's story. When she and Naomi made the trek to Bethlehem-judah, they ran into a distant relative to Elimelech—Boaz. The story of their meeting and eventual marriage is beautiful enough. But look closely at the very end of the book:

Ruth 4:13-22:

13 So Boaz took Ruth, and she was his wife: and when he went in unto her, the Lord gave her conception, and she bare a son.

14 And the women said unto Naomi, Blessed be the Lord, which hath not left thee this day without a kinsman, that his name may be famous in Israel.

15 And he shall be unto thee a restorer of thy life, and a nourisher of thine old age: for thy daughter in law, which loveth thee, which is better to thee than seven sons, hath born him.

16 And Naomi took the child, and laid it in her bosom, and became nurse unto it.

17 And the women her neighbours gave it a name, saying, There is a son born to Naomi; and they called his name Obed: he is the father of Jesse, the father of David.

18 Now these are the generations of Pharez: Pharez begat Hezron,

19 And Hezron begat Ram, and Ram begat Amminadab,

20 And Amminadab begat Nahshon, and Nahshon begat Salmon,

21 And Salmon begat Boaz, and Boaz begat Obed,

22 And Obed begat Jesse, and Jesse begat David.

Wait…excuse me? Ruth gives birth to Obed. Obed becomes the father of Jesse. Jesse becomes the father…of **KING DAVID**? Let that sink in. Ruth's decision to follow the God of her mother-in-law resulted in her giving birth to one of the greatest biblical kings ever—with a direct lineage to the King of Kings!

I doubt that this was part of Ruth or Naomi's agenda when they left Moab. They moved having only their love for each other and their love for a God they could not see—who was ordering their steps all along. Most of all, Ruth was willing to make big, faith-filled moves. And as a result, she was not only blessed, but gave birth to a blessing.

It makes you wonder. What will your "yes" give birth to?

Now, let's look at the story of Abraham's call.

Genesis 12 recounts how Abraham was first approached by the Lord. In this case, he was asked to leave his country, kindred and father's house to go to the land that God would show him. He's also told that the Lord would make him a "great nation" and that he would be blessed. So at the age of 75, Abraham does just as he was instructed; he and his family leave his native country of Haran and go where God instructed him. I mean, it sounds like a great package to me right? If he simply obeys and follows God wherever He takes him, not only would he be blessed, but his future lineage would be as well.

Now if you read on, you realize that Abraham's promise took a while—years in fact. Which made the promise that was made so many years before seem almost…well…expired. I'm sure he asked himself, "OK, why did I leave home again?" However, God came back to encourage Abraham in Genesis 15: 1-6 that the promise was still good. He was definitely going to be blessed:

Genesis 15: 1-6:

1 After these things the word of the Lord came unto Abram in a vision, saying, Fear not, Abram: I am thy shield, and thy exceeding great reward.

2 And Abram said, Lord God, what wilt thou give me, seeing I go childless, and the steward of my house is this Eliezer of Damascus?

3 And Abram said, Behold, to me thou hast given no seed: and, lo, one born in my house is mine heir.

4 And, behold, the word of the Lord came unto him, saying, This shall not be thine heir; but he that shall come forth out of thine own bowels shall be thine heir.

5 And he brought him forth abroad, and said, Look now toward heaven, and tell the stars, if thou be able to number them: and he said unto him, So shall thy seed be.

6 And he believed in the Lord; and he counted it to him for righteousness.

God said it. He believed it. That settled it! Well…almost. You see, although Abraham (previously Abram) was reassured that he was on track for gaining an heir and blessings, he and his wife Sarah decide to help God out. Now remember, God Himself said that this was going to be a done deal. However, Abraham and Sarah looked at their situation as impossible because in their eyes, they knew they were really old. Sarah figured there was no way she could have a baby at this point, so she gave her handmaiden, Hagar, to Abraham so that they could have his future heir through her. I don't have to tell you how that worked out. (By the way, reading some of the stories in the Old Testament can rival any reality show.) As expected, Sarah became jealous when Hagar gave birth to Ishmael. But they didn't need to go that route in the first place. If Sarah and Abraham had just waited, they would have seen that God wasn't going back on His word. Yes they were old, but in the end Sarah gave birth to God's promise: Isaac. How old were they when that happened? Abraham was 100 and Sarah was around 90.

What is the lesson here? First, we know that God does not lie. If He says that He will do something, we have to trust that it's coming to pass. Second, if we look at Abraham's story, the circumstances may seem extreme. We can see that Abraham had to move far and wait long for his calling. I'm pretty certain that Abraham and Sarah thought that Isaac would have arrived much earlier. But I believe God had a purpose even in this. We know that Abraham's calling was that he was going to be blessed greatly if he continued to follow God's lead. However, I think there was one more blessing in the deal that he and Sarah (who was originally named Sarai) probably weren't expecting. Abraham didn't just have to move further physically. He had to move further in his faith as well. I believe that God allowed the years to go by so that Abraham's faith would increase—thereby making him ready for whatever tests would come his way afterwards. I know that in my own life, the stretching that I have experienced through various tests—and long waiting periods—has allowed me to give birth to increased faith as a result.

Please understand that your blessing *will* come at His appointed time. You just have to keep moving forward until it manifests. If He said it, then trust that it's happening. And when you get to where you're supposed to be, you can rejoice in the fact that not only did you achieve your purpose. You have now gained precious wisdom that you can share with others who are on their own journey to their purpose.

LESSON 5:

...AND YOU MAY HAVE TO MOVE QUICKLY!

Elisha's Story

Scripture: 1 Kings 19:19-21

I want to talk just a little bit about the speed in which you may be called to your assignment. It may surprise you! The question is: will you be ready, willing and able to make a move when the time comes?

Many of us have had dreams and inklings about where God has called us to. Unfortunately, not all of us have acted on it. We come up with every excuse in the book to put it off. I don't have time. I wouldn't be good at this. So many people can do this better than me. I don't have enough influence or followers. Pretty soon, you're used to giving excuses...and time continues to march on. Days turn into months, months turn into years and then decades. Before you know it, it's thirty years later. And still...you haven't produced or walked into what you were called to do so many years ago.

Now don't get me wrong...I believe that as long as you're breathing, you have life! Some of our greatest inventions and products were launched by those well into their 40's, 50's, 60's and even later. Vera Wang opened her first bridal boutique after deciding she wanted to be a designer at age 40. Sam Walton was 42 when he opened the first Walmart. Yes, sometimes your destiny manifests later in life. What I will point out is the common thread for all of them: they simply got started. They took the first step and kept moving! Even if they stopped for a bit along the way—whether it was figuring out how to balance a family, finding funding for a project or tweaking some aspects of their business plan—they did not press pause forever. And when they moved again, it was towards an expected end.

So, you may have to move quicker than you expected and be ready to just keep it moving. Which brings me to the story of Elisha.

When we first meet him, the prophet Elijah (not to be confused with Elisha...yes, I know) finds him plowing with twelve yoke of oxen. He's only mentioned a few verses earlier in 1 Kings 19:16. That's when the Lord has to give Elijah a pep talk after he's running scared from threats made by Jezebel—the wife of King Ahab. The Lord tells him not to fear and to anoint men such as Elisha and others who would back him up if things ever got crazy. So upon finding him, Elijah threw his cloak around him—which was essentially "the call" for him. There wasn't a long drawn out ceremony. Most of all, there wasn't a lot of time for Elisha to make a decision:

1 Kings 19:19-21:

19 So he departed thence, and found Elisha the son of Shaphat, who was plowing with twelve yoke of oxen before him, and he with the twelfth: and Elijah passed by him, and cast his mantle upon him.

20 And he left the oxen, and ran after Elijah, and said, Let me, I pray thee, kiss my father and my mother, and then I will follow thee. And he said unto him, Go back again: for what have I done to thee?

21 And he returned back from him, and took a yoke of oxen, and slew them, and boiled their flesh with the instruments of the oxen, and gave unto the people, and they did eat. Then he arose, and went after Elijah, and ministered unto him.

Well that was quick! One minute, Elisha was minding his business. The next minute, he's Elijah's right-hand man. Here's how the Message Version describes Elijah's words to Elisha in verse 20:

"Go ahead," said Elijah, "but, mind you, don't forget what I've just done to you."

I love how Elisha paused only to say goodbye to his parents, and then he was ready to hit the road with his new mentor. He didn't dismiss the urgency in the call when Elijah told him, "don't forget what I've just done to you." He somehow knew that there was no turning back.

That's how fast it can happen for you. The change that you've been waiting for can come quickly. The question is, will you be ready? You've been praying that someone would hear the song you wrote, and then you get a DM from a producer who wants to connect after they saw the video you posted. The blog that you've been writing suddenly catches the attention of a major book publisher. You don't know who's watching you. And one more thing…

Start practicing your "yes." Again, Elisha didn't play around with this new assignment. As you read on, you'll see that when Elijah knew that it was time for him to die, Elisha was blessed with a "double portion" of his mentor's anointing:

<u>2 Kings 2:1-15:</u>

1 And it came to pass, when the Lord would take up Elijah into heaven by a whirlwind, that Elijah went with Elisha from Gilgal.

2 And Elijah said unto Elisha, Tarry here, I pray thee; for the Lord hath sent me to Bethel. And Elisha said unto him, As the Lord liveth, and as thy soul liveth, I will not leave thee. So they went down to Bethel.

3 And the sons of the prophets that were at Bethel came forth to Elisha, and said unto him, Knowest thou that the Lord will take away thy master from thy head to day? And he said, Yea, I know it; hold ye your peace.

4 And Elijah said unto him, Elisha, tarry here, I pray thee; for the Lord hath sent me to Jericho. And he said, As the Lord liveth, and as thy soul liveth, I will not leave thee. So they came to Jericho.

5 And the sons of the prophets that were at Jericho came to Elisha, and said unto him, Knowest thou that the Lord will take away thy master from thy head to day? And he answered, Yea, I know it; hold ye your peace.

6 And Elijah said unto him, Tarry, I pray thee, here; for the Lord hath sent me to Jordan. And he said, As the Lord liveth, and as thy soul liveth, I will not leave thee. And they two went on.

7 And fifty men of the sons of the prophets went, and stood to view afar off: and they two stood by Jordan.

8 And Elijah took his mantle, and wrapped it together, and smote the waters, and they were divided hither and thither, so that they two went over on dry ground.

9 And it came to pass, when they were gone over, that Elijah said unto Elisha, Ask what I shall do for thee, before I be taken away from thee. And Elisha said, I pray thee, let a double portion of thy spirit be upon me.

10 And he said, Thou hast asked a hard thing: nevertheless, if thou see me when I am taken from thee, it shall be so unto thee; but if not, it shall not be so.

11 And it came to pass, as they still went on, and talked, that, behold, there appeared a chariot of fire, and horses of fire, and parted them both asunder; and Elijah went up by a whirlwind into heaven.

12 And Elisha saw it, and he cried, My father, my father, the chariot of Israel, and the horsemen thereof. And he saw him no more: and he took hold of his own clothes, and rent them in two pieces.

13 He took up also the mantle of Elijah that fell from him, and went back, and stood by the bank of Jordan;

14 And he took the mantle of Elijah that fell from him, and smote the waters, and said, Where is the Lord God of Elijah? and when he also

had smitten the waters, they parted hither and thither: and Elisha went over.

15 And when the sons of the prophets which were to view at Jericho saw him, they said, The spirit of Elijah doth rest on Elisha. And they came to meet him, and bowed themselves to the ground before him.

All of this. Just from one "yes"…

I pray that by the time you finished reading this book, you will not only see open doors, but you will also pray for an open heart and mind that is ready to say "yes" to the call and assignment that is on your life, in Jesus name!

LESSON 6:
BE PREPARED TO SACRIFICE SOMETHING

Hannah's story

Scripture: 1 Samuel 1: 25-26

One biblical story that I believe perfectly demonstrates how to recognize one's true assignment is the story of Hannah, the mother of the prophet Samuel (I mentioned him during the story of David in Lesson 1.)

There are so many layers to Hannah's journey. First off, her call was birthed out of her strong desire for a son. Meaning, she probably wouldn't have thought to go the route she did if this challenge wasn't set before her. You see, 1 Samuel chapter 1 tells us that, while Hannah was happily married to her husband Elkanah, she was sore at the fact that she was not able to give him a male child. What made it worse was that his other wife, Penninah, was popping out babies left and right! Then, she even had the nerve to rub it in Hannah's face. Interestingly, when the bible references Hannah's condition, it states that it was God who had "shut up her womb."

Ummm...what? Here she is praying, serving and believing that her circumstance would change. But God was the one who actually blocked it? Once again, I want you to walk in her shoes for a minute. What happens when you're trying to achieve success, make moves, move up the ladder...but you know that something clearly is in the way? I'm sure the question most of us would ask is: "Lord, if you know that I want this, then why are you allowing this to be so hard? This really hurts!" Hannah had reached a breaking point. It was no longer business as usual. I believe that she began to realize that her request—and her purpose—was not just going to be ordinary. So, she decided to sacrifice something in order to achieve her true calling and purpose. And when she finally recognized that, her situation finally changed:

<u>1 Samuel 1:9-11:</u>

9 So Hannah rose up after they had eaten in Shiloh, and after they had drunk. Now Eli the priest sat upon a seat by a post of the temple of the Lord.

10 And she was in bitterness of soul, and prayed unto the Lord, and wept sore.

11 And she vowed a vow, and said, O Lord of hosts, if thou wilt indeed look on the affliction of thine handmaid, and remember me, and not forget thine handmaid, but wilt give unto thine handmaid a man child, then I will give him unto the Lord all the days of his life, and there shall no razor come upon his head.

Whoa! She really "went in" didn't she? She finally realized that she had to approach God in a different way in order to get this special calling. She no longer just wanted to be a mother. She was willing to give her baby back to the Lord.

Let's look at that for a minute. She clearly wanted to have a child—she cried about it, went to sleep thinking about it, and tried to get her husband to understand how she felt not being able to have a child for him. However, she realized that only God could deliver this blessing. What would she offer up to God in return? The answer came to her: A child dedicated to the Lord's service. And of course, we know that Samuel would become one of the greatest prophets of Israel. By the way...she wound up having more children after that!

She made good on her promise: she made a huge sacrifice by letting Samuel live with the prophet Eli. I'm sure young Samuel didn't understand why he couldn't be with his precious mother. And I know Hannah's heart was overwhelmed when she had to leave him with Eli. But a vow is a vow: if God would give her and Elkanah the child she prayed for, she would gladly let him be used for the Lord's service all his days. She had to let go of her idea of what her life should look like, and instead she asked God to paint the picture that He wanted. And it turned out to be better than she could ever imagine.

I want to say to you that if it feels like God is allowing your pathway to be blocked for a season, then you need to ask yourself the question: what do I need to give up or sacrifice? Although it won't be as hard as Hannah's choice, you should fast and pray about it. Could it be that, instead of going for that new job or promotion, there's a ministry that He wants to birth within you instead? You may be thinking your church auxiliary role was where you would stay for years, but is He calling you to another area of the vineyard to serve Him?

I know that God is able to do the miraculous. Whenever I hear of someone battling a huge challenge such as a disease or calamity, I have no doubt that the Lord is able to heal and deliver them. I realized that some challenges are a test of our faith. Then there are other times…when He wants something birthed out of us.

Here's the catch: in order to recognize which of these scenarios applies to you, you really have to take a step back and listen to Him. And then…wait for the answer. If you are in what seems to be a "blocking season," ask how you can use what you have for His kingdom. Are you asking for wealth, whether through multiple streams or a higher paying job? Then, what's your plan for helping your family or community once you receive it? Are you asking Him to bless your gift of singing or writing? How will you use that to be a blessing and to reach the lost or the hurting?

You see, at the end of the day, your calling really isn't about you. It's all about Him and the Kingdom. Sure, there are blessings along the way because of our obedience to His call. However, learn to worry less about what you're getting, and instead focus on what you're giving that will help others.

As we learned from all of these examples, you never know what your call will give birth to. Yes, it may cost you something. You may have to move far, and you may have to move quickly. It may not be comfortable for you. But remember, nothing will be wasted—He will use it all.

Now, my friend, the rest is up to you...

LESSON 7: LAST CALL

As I prepare to end this book, I would be remiss to not speak of the one call that is available to all. It is the call of Salvation.

I mentioned earlier that I have experienced over twenty-five years working within the public relations industry. Now, it usually won't take that long to find your call or assignment! But I will tell you that whether it's 25 years or 25 minutes, you will need the Lord Jesus Christ to guide your footsteps. Let me explain…

Similar to finding the proverbial final piece to the puzzle, having the Lord to guide your life will be the answer to your questions when you find yourself at life's crossroad. Whether it's deciding where to go to school, where to find a job, where to move, who to marry…trust me when I tell you that you want heavenly guidance before you take the next step.

Remember all of the examples that I shared? Each person realized that, unless the Lord was on their side, they would not have achieved true success or found their purpose. I'd even venture to say that none of them would have even realized that there was a void in their life, if He hadn't somehow tapped them on the shoulder to eventually reveal it to them.

My hope is that's what He will do for you now, as you read these words. You may have been used to living life in a way that's just "business as usual." But these are not "business as usual" times. Between watching the news or scrolling your social timeline, there is just so much that we are dealing with right now. However, whether you are experiencing a global pandemic or a family crisis, you should know that all problems great and small can be surrendered to Him. Just make Him Lord of your life:

<u>*John 3:16:*</u>

16 For God so loved the world, that he gave his only begotten Son, that whosoever believeth in him should not perish, but have everlasting life.

<u>*Acts 2:38:*</u>

38 Then Peter said unto them, Repent, and be baptized every one of you in the name of Jesus Christ for the remission of sins, and ye shall receive the gift of the Holy Ghost.

You may wonder why I would take the time out here to even bring this up. "Sheila, I thought this book was for those who feel unsure of their calling?" Well, it is. Take it from someone who has been on this walk for a while— you don't want to do this alone.

The process of finding your purpose and assignment doesn't have to be a solo effort. Sure, it is good to have wise counsel in your corner to bounce things off of and to offer guidance along the way. But you definitely need the Wonderful Counselor to be in full control of ordering your steps. Trust me, you want this type of security as God takes you to new heights and paths.

I believe that there is a great work that is going to be birthed in you (and in me!) Remember the testimonies of those I shared in this book if you ever begin to doubt. And be ready to help the next generation that's on their way.

It's time for your calling to be revealed!

PRAISE FOR THE AUTHOR

"Sheila Harris, a longtime force for change in publishing and a public relations strategist, has written a revolutionary, life-changing view on the price of success and its sustainability using biblical legends as her template. The book is like having 'Coach Harris' in your ear, navigating you on the journey called life and believe me, the insights are priceless!" -*Mikki Taylor, Author, Speaker, Executive Producer, Satin Doll Films*

"*Calling Revealed: 7 Spiritual Lessons to Uncover Your Purpose* is the book for this appointed time. As we come through one of the most uncertain times we've ever experience, Sheila Harris reminds us through this book that God intends for us to rise out of this and walk in His calling. This book is for anyone at a crossroads in life or for anyone who wants to truly uncover their purpose and live in God's promise. That's basically everyone! *Calling Revealed* is an inspiring call to action. It's an easy read, with applicable stories and examples that will give you the motivation to write your vision, make it plain and live your dreams." -*Kayla Tucker Adams, Public Relations Executive, KTA Media Group*

"*Calling Revealed: 7 Spiritual Lessons to Uncover Your Purpose* was life-changing. As believers, there are times when we all have to ask ourselves the question: what is my purpose? Through stories of different people who were called by God, we see how He can use our pain for a purpose. This book showed me that your calling may come at a price, but the return on investment is well worth it." -*Cameka Smith, Founder of The BOSS Network*

ABOUT THE AUTHOR

Sheila Harris is an author, speaker and Certified John Maxwell Life Coach. She offers a message of empowerment and faith as she speaks at schools, organizations and churches—teaching audiences how to tap into their passions and to walk into their God-given destiny.

Sheila is also a communications industry veteran who has served the majority of her career at ESSENCE Magazine. During her twenty-plus year tenure there, she has led publicity campaigns for many of its top-tiered events and initiatives. Over the years, she has been involved with various community and faith-based initiatives. She has also served her church—the historic Harlem-based Greater Refuge Temple—in various ministries including within its youth department, choir, broadcast ministry, trustee board and more. Follow her on Instagram @SistaSheilaSays for more inspiring content.

www.ingramcontent.com/pod-product-compliance
Lightning Source LLC
Chambersburg PA
CBHW030508220526
45464CB00006B/2706